SETTLEMENT HOUSES

Improving the Social Welfare of America's Immigrants

Michael Friedman and
Brett Friedman

rosen central
Primary Source ™

The Rosen Publishing Group, Inc., New York

For Mom and Dad

Published in 2006 by The Rosen Publishing Group, Inc.
29 East 21st Street, New York, NY 10010

Copyright © 2006 by The Rosen Publishing Group, Inc.

First Edition

Library of Congress Cataloging-in-Publication Data

Friedman, Michael
Settlement houses : improving the social welfare of America's immigrants / Michael Friedman and Brett Friedman—1st ed.
    p. cm.—(The progressive movement 1900–1920: efforts to reform America's new industrial society)
Includes bibliographical references and index.
ISBN 1-4042-0194-7 (lib. bdg.)
ISBN 1-4042-0859-3 (pbk. bdg.)
6-pack ISBN 1-4042-6194-X
1. Social settlements—United States—History—Juvenile literature. 2. Immigrants—Services for—United States—History—Juvenile literature. 3. Women in charitable work—United States—History—Juvenile literature.
I. Friedman, Brett. II. Title. III. Series.
HV4194.F75 2005
362.8—dc22
                                                                                    2004002684

Manufactured in the United States of America

On the cover: Top: Three boys sleeping on a doorstep in New York City in 1888, as photographed by writer and social activist Jacob A. Riis. Bottom: Chicago's Hull House in the early 1900s

Photo credits: cover (top), pp. 8, 14, 26 Library of Congress Prints and Photographs Division; cover (bottom) Barnes-Crosby/Chicago Historical Society; p. 5 courtesy of George Eastman House; p. 6 Special Collections, University Library, University of Illinois at Chicago; p. 10 National Archives; p. 13 Rare Book, Manuscript, and Special Collections Library, Duke University; pp. 13 (inset), 27 © Hulton Archive/Getty Images; pp. 15, 17 Swarthmore College Peace Collection; p. 19 courtesy of Wellesley College Archives, photo by Seaver; p. 21 The Western Reserve Historical Society Library; p. 23 courtesy of the Visiting Nurse Service of New York; p. 24 © Bettmann/Corbis.

Designer: Les Kanturek; Editor: Joann Jovinelly; Photo Researcher: Amy Feinberg

Contents

Chapter One

Society's Ills

After the Civil War (1861–1865), the growth of the United States extended farther west. Pioneers settled less populated territories in search of better lives. They founded new towns and expanded existing towns into cities.

This westward movement fueled incredible growth in the business world. There were railroads to build and engines to fuel. The United States needed new buildings, new clothes, and new tools. Huge companies like Carnegie Steel and Standard Oil were formed. Men became millionaires in industries like transportation, manufacturing, and banking.

Inexpensive labor was needed to man the country's factories. There were more job openings than people to fill them. The United States answered this need by opening its doors to immigrants from Europe. Almost 12 million new

This Italian family was photographed leaving Ellis Island, New York, in 1905. About 17 million European and Asian immigrants obtained permission to enter the United States through Ellis Island between 1892 and 1924. Today, Ellis Island houses a museum dedicated to educating others about the immigrant experience in America.

citizens came to America's shores between 1890 and 1910. Most of them were Italian, Russian, or Irish.

Many immigrants settled in the large cities of the Northeast. New York and Boston became home to thousands of newcomers. St. Louis, then known as the Gateway to the West, also received many new faces. At

Fire escapes can be seen in this 1916 photograph of the rear section of a tenement apartment in Chicago. The lighting and air circulation were so poor in tenement dwellings that inhabitants were often forced to eat and work outside. Fire escapes provided the opportunity to get much-needed daylight and fresh air.

first, immigrant families couldn't afford their own apartments. They were forced to live together in crowded buildings called tenements. Life for immigrant families was difficult. The tenements were often dark environments, with few windows and poor air circulation. Their neighborhoods were troubled by crime. Garbage piled up in the streets, spreading disease.

The immigrants had expected to find a land of opportunity. What they found instead were demanding factory jobs, long hours, and often crippling working conditions. They could barely get by on their modest wages. Often, their children had to work to help pay the bills.

Unfortunately, city governments didn't do much to help their new citizens. Politicians were more interested in piling up votes than actually helping the poor. Many of them took bribes from the well-to-do. Most of the time, services such as firefighting and policing were supplied only to middle-class

Jacob Riis

Before 1900, living conditions in downtown New York City were terrible. Most people in the United States were unaware of these problems until a writer named Jacob Riis documented them. He was a crusading journalist, known as a muckraker.

In 1890, Riis published a book called *How the Other Half Lives*, which profiled the lifestyles of Lower East Side immigrants. Riis described how they slept in rundown, overcrowded tenement buildings often riddled with disease. More important, he was among the first people to photograph these conditions.

Riis's book forced New York City's government to improve its tenements. *How the Other Half Lives* made a difference in the lives of New York City's immigrants.

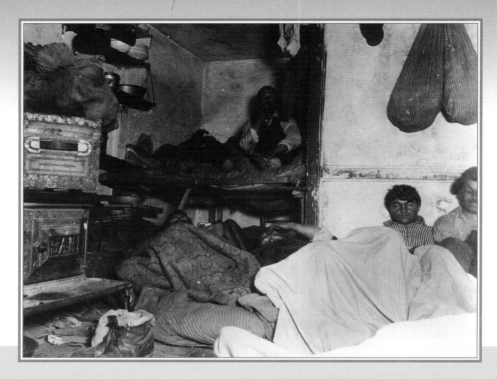

Jacob A. Riis (1849–1914), a New York reporter and social activist, took this photograph of immigrants sleeping in an illegal tenement apartment in New York in 1890. Riis, an immigrant himself who came to the United States from Denmark, wrote *How the Other Half Lives*, a book that described New York City slums. Immigrants were often forced to live in poor conditions. Riis's documentation, in both writing and photography, helped lead to widespread social reforms.

neighborhoods, while immigrant neighborhoods were lucky to get any protection at all. Without power or money, immigrants were all but forgotten. It seemed as though these newcomers had nowhere to turn.

Chapter Two

The Progressive Movement

ome people saw the arrival of European immigrants as a threat to their American way of life. After all, the newcomers looked and dressed differently. They spoke their own languages and followed their own customs. Americans didn't know if the immigrants could be trusted. They came from faraway places with strange-sounding names. Many had never lived in a democracy. Americans wondered if the immigrants would remain loyal to their former countries.

Fortunately for the newcomers, other Americans believed in them. They argued that immigrants had the ability to be useful members of society. All they needed was a little help. The Americans who wished to provide that help were called reformers. Reformers were thought to be liberal-minded, or progressive. Because of them, the period from approximately 1900 to 1920 is called the Progressive Era.

Pushcart vendors and bands of immigrant families crowded New York's Lower East Side in this photograph taken on Hester Street in 1903. The majority of immigrants who stayed in New York after arriving on Ellis Island formed concentrated ethnic neighborhoods. More than 80,000 people immigrated to New York in 1889, many of whom would reside in the city's more than 30,000 tenement dwellings.

During the age of reform between the Civil War and the Great Depression (late 1920s to early 1930s), much progress was made to improve the economy and politics of the United States. Activists helped decrease child labor practices, long work hours, and unfit living conditions in American cities. Muckraking journalists such as Lincoln Steffens exposed the American people corporate excesses, such as those of Standard Oil, which had developed into a monopoly. In 1920, the Nineteenth Amendment was passed, which gave women the right to vote. Within a few years, city and state activists of the Progressive movement had national allies, including Presidents Woodrow Wilson and Franklin D. Roosevelt.

Most of all, reformers changed the face of the United States with their work on the behalf of the poor and the powerless. They became the voice of those who could not speak English. And one of their biggest contributions to immigrants was the creation of the settlement house.

Chapter Three

The Settlement House

Toynbee Hall, the world's first settlement house, was established in 1884. But it wasn't in the United States. It was located in the slums of the East End in London, England. Samuel A. Barnett, the founder of Toynbee Hall, was a clergyman. Barnett's idea was for university students to settle in a house in a poor neighborhood. This would give them a chance to lift the spirits of the people who lived there. The students would also learn something about the real world.

Several Americans were inspired by Toynbee Hall. One of them was Stanton Coit. In 1886, he established Neighborhood Guild (now University Settlement), in New York City. In 1889, a group of young college women founded another settlement house in New York. They called it the College Settlement. Two years later, Andover

Samuel Augustus Barnett and Henrietta Barnett *(inset)* established Toynbee Hall, the first settlement house, in London's East End in 1884. Named after the nineteenth-century social reformer Arnold Toynbee, Toynbee Hall continues to serve Londoners today with legal advice, welfare assistance, and teaching services for immigrants.

THE PUBLIC HEALTH NURSE

She Answers Humanity's Call

Your Red Cross Membership makes her work possible

This twentieth-century poster urged citizens to join the American Red Cross during a membership drive. Female public health nurses, like the one pictured in the poster, answered the calls of people living in over-crowded cities, where outbreaks of smallpox, influenza, and cholera were frequent.

House (now South End House) was established in Boston.

Six years later, Lillian Wald founded the Henry Street Settlement on the Lower East Side. Wald had seen the immigrants' problems with disease as a student at the Women's Medical College in New York. She introduced the idea of public health nursing. Her goal was to make medical care available to everyone who needed it. Perhaps the most famous settlement house was Hull House. It was located in an old mansion on Chicago's West Side. Hull House was founded in 1889 by Jane Addams and Ellen Starr, both graduates of Rockford Female Seminary, now Rockford College.

Settlement houses eased and brightened the lives of the immigrants they served. They did this by providing nurseries, libraries, and theaters. They supplied space for social

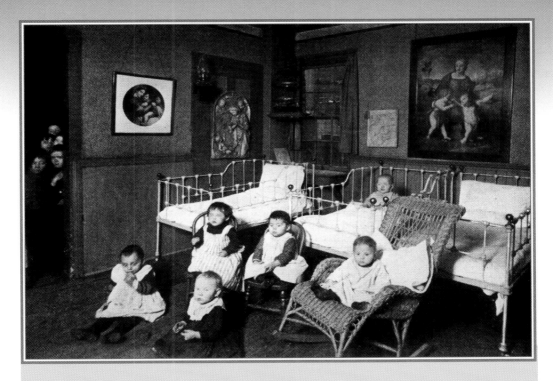

These children resided in Chicago's Hull House settlement in the 1890s. Jane Addams founded Hull House in 1889 after she visited England's Toynbee Hall and witnessed a group of university students assisting impoverished residents of London's East End. When it was first established, Hull House included a kindergarten, a nursery, and a day-care center.

clubs and discussion groups. The settlement houses also helped immigrants act more like Americans. It wasn't just a matter of teaching them English. Immigrants also learned music, art, and job skills. They learned how to run a home and obtain health care.

Jane Addams of Hull House

Although Jane Addams came from a middle-class background, she believed that she had a duty to help the poor. After she graduated college, she visited Toynbee Hall in England, where she was inspired to become a social worker. In 1889, a wealthy man named Charles Hull gave Addams an old mansion in a Chicago slum. Addams and her college friend Ellen Gates Starr turned it into a settlement house. Immigrants flocked to Hull House. Some of them later became famous, such as Benny Goodman, a clarinet player and bandleader of the 1930s and 1940s.

Addams believed that everyone, including immigrants, deserved dignity and respect. Most of all, Addams wanted to help people help themselves. Addams died in 1935, but even after her death, the residents of Hull House carried on her work.

The hardest immigrants to attract were men, so settlement house establishers created basketball leagues. Once the men were engaged in one program, they often stayed to learn other things. It took money to offer these programs. Also, the buildings themselves had to be maintained. Settlement house expenses were often paid with the help of private donations and, in some cases, support from religious groups. However, the settlements didn't pay their residents a salary. The men and women who lived there worked for free. In some cases, they even paid rent.

Residents came from financially stable backgrounds and were often college-educated. They had bright futures in a range of different professions. Yet they gave up their personal comfort and safety to live in the settlements. They dedicated themselves to a difficult task: solving the problems of the immigrants.

The settlement house idea spread quickly throughout the United States. By 1897, there were seventy-four such institu-

Jane Addams (1860–1935), an activist and writer, was a pioneer in the field of social work. Her devotion to Chicago's immigrant population, its minorities, and its poor was unrivaled in her work at Hull House, a settlement house that cared for the hungry, sick, and misguided.

tions. Three years later, there were more than 100. By 1915, there were more than 400. Most of them sprang up in large cities. Four out of ten settlement houses were in New York, Boston, or Chicago. However, many small cities and towns eventually had settlement houses too.

Chapter Four

The Rise of Women

Women played a large role in the settlement house movement. This was because of the simultaneous rise of women's colleges in the United States. These institutions were established in the late nineteenth century, and they were the first to allow women to take part in the process of higher learning.

In the nineteenth century, most American women were expected to become wives and mothers. In that role, they raised children and performed household tasks like cooking and sewing. If they didn't marry, they often faced a lonely life on their own. Even single women were limited in what they could do for a living. Most couldn't become doctors or lawyers. They couldn't enter the world of business. Nursing and teaching were among the few careers open to them.

Some women wanted to do more with what they had learned in college. Working in settlement houses offered

These young women are studying mathematics in the early 1900s. During this time, many educated, upper-class women decided to work toward social reforms. Their combined efforts led to many of the changes that took place during the Progressive movement, such as the passage of the Nineteenth Amendment that gave women the right to vote, labor laws and legislature that protected the rights and welfare of adults and children, and improved social conditions in America's cities.

African American Settlements

Thousands of African Americans moved to American cities between 1890 and 1915. They had much in common with European immigrants since they were also in an unfamiliar place with little money. African American immigrants needed to learn job skills and typical American customs. They also needed the advantages that nurseries, health care, and libraries could provide.

And while settlement houses like Hull House helped Europeans, they were segregated. African Americans had no choice but to open their own settlement houses. Like white settlements, they were run by educated, middle-class women. However, these women were of African American descent.

Ida B. Wells-Barnett, a former slave, was a leader in Chicago's African American community. She founded the Negro Fellowship League, a settlement house for homeless men. Jane Edna Hunter, another African American, established the Phillis Wheatley Home in Cleveland, Ohio, in 1911, which was named after a slave who became a published poet. Spurred by its success, similar settlements opened in other cities.

The settlement house movement later grew to include services for children such as day care and helped form laws that regulated child labor, juvenile courts, mothers' pensions, and workers' compensation.

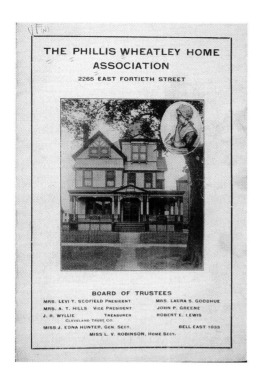

This circular shows a photograph of the Phillis Wheatley Home, a settlement house in Cleveland, Ohio, that was named after a Boston slave (*inset*) who became an educated writer and poet. The Phillis Wheatley Home was founded in 1911 by Jane Edna Hunter (1882–1971), a nurse and reformer who dedicated her life to improve the lives of single African American women.

women increased opportunities. It was a chance to put their education and skills to good use. As residents in settlement houses, women were able to take part in the reform movement. They were also able to find stimulating companionship among their fellow residents. Settlements didn't just help immigrants make the most of their lives. They also helped empower educated women.

Chapter Five

Settlement Houses' Mark on Society

Settlement houses were created to help immigrants meet the challenges of living in America. They helped our country's newest citizens survive and prosper. They also led the way for the reform movement. People like Jane Addams and Lillian Wald spoke out against social injustice. They convinced others that it was their duty to help the needy. The federal government passed laws protecting adult and juvenile workers. Little by little, immigrant families gained acceptance among other Americans. Their customs were celebrated instead of frowned upon. They were woven into the fabric of the United States.

But it wasn't only the immigrants whose lives were changed. Places like Hull House and Henry Street Settlement also changed the lives of the men and women

This woman, seen climbing over tenement rooftops to make a house call in 1909, was a public nurse employed by the Visiting Nurse Service of New York. Lillian D. Wald (1867–1940) started the service in 1893 from the Henry Street Settlement, which she also founded. In 1912, Wald helped found and became the president of the National Organization of Public Health Nursing.

who lived there. They were encouraged to take the spirit of reform beyond the settlement houses and into immigrant communities.

Settlement residents pressed for fair pay and for workers' compensation laws to protect injured workers. They spoke

Eleanor Roosevelt (1884–1962), first lady and wife of former President Franklin D. Roosevelt, is seen dishing out meals to unemployed women at a Grand Central restaurant in New York City in 1932. Eleanor Roosevelt spent her entire life working as a humanitarian and advocate for improved housing, child welfare, and womens' rights.

out against the cruelty of child labor. They campaigned to improve housing for the poor. They also helped establish parks, playgrounds, and community centers.

At the time, women were not allowed to vote in government elections. Settlement houses and their residents also

Eleanor Roosevelt

Eleanor Roosevelt came from a wealthy family in New York City. In 1902, at the age of eighteen, she volunteered in a settlement house and entered the reform movement.

Eleanor married her cousin, Franklin D. Roosevelt, in 1905 and continued fighting for justice. When the United States entered World War I in 1917, Eleanor worked for the American Red Cross. Franklin Roosevelt served as a state senator from 1910 to 1913, and Eleanor worked for his social programs. Later, Franklin Roosevelt became governor of New York and then, in 1933, president of the United States.

Eleanor traveled around the country. She gave lectures and radio broadcasts and even wrote a newspaper column called "My Day." From 1945 through 1953, Eleanor represented the United States in the United Nations, and in 1946, she became the chairperson of the UN Human Rights Commission. Eleanor favored the causes of women's rights and African American equality. For her tireless efforts, she became one of the most beloved Americans of her time.

fought hard to change that. Finally, on August 26, 1920, laws were passed that allowed U.S. women to vote.

Even after they left the settlements, many settlement house residents continued to serve the poor and the powerless. Florence Kelley became director of the National Consumers' League, protecting people from uncaring

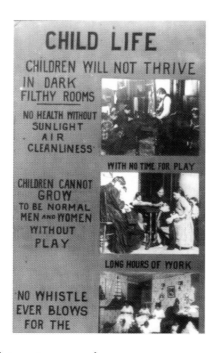

This nineteenth-century poster educated people about the dangers of children living in the tenement slums of America's cities.

businessmen. Julia Lathrop became the first director of the Children's Bureau. Grace Abbott became the director of the Immigrants' Protective League. Alice Hamilton, a resident of Hull House, was the first woman to become a professor at Harvard Medical School.

The settlement movement also gave birth to a new field called social work. Sophonisba Breckinridge and Edith Abbott both became leaders in this field. Both of them were originally residents of settlement houses.

Other settlement residents became active in government. Frances Perkins and Harry Hopkins helped President Franklin D. Roosevelt with his New Deal ideas in the 1930s, along with his wife, Eleanor Roosevelt, who had also been a settlement house volunteer.

In time, settlement houses began to change. Some of them vanished when immigrant neighborhoods were rebuilt in the 1940s and 1950s. Others closed because of

A banner reading "Votes for Women" advertises a talk about womens' suffrage given by Jane Addams and other social reformers at Carnegie Hall in New York in 1913. Within seven years, in 1920, the Nineteenth Amendment was passed, giving women the same rights to vote as men.

insufficient funds. Still others became neighborhood centers, with paid employees taking the place of residents.

Today, settlement houses may be difficult to recognize. Although they might be known by different names, hundreds of them survive. They continue to provide services for the elderly, the poor, and those in need of a helping hand.

Glossary

abolish (uh-BAH-lish) To do away with.

democracy (di-MAH-kruh-see) A system of government whereby people choose leaders and participate in making laws through an election process.

Great Depression (GRAYT dih-PREH-shun) A period of American history during the late 1920s and early 1930s when businesses lost money and there were few jobs.

Hull House (HUL HOWS) Among the first social settlement houses in America, located in Chicago and founded in 1889 by Jane Addams and Ellen Gates Starr.

immigrant (IH-muh-grint) Someone who moves to a new country from another country.

Immigrants' Protective League (IH-muh-grints pruh-TEKT-ehv LEEG) A nineteenth-century organization in Chicago, Illinois, headed by Grace Abbott that fought against the exploitation of immigrants.

injustice (in-JUS-tis) The absence of justice; the act of being unfair.

monopolies (muh-NAH-puh-leez) Businesses owned by one group that grew large enough to fix prices and dominate industries by destroying competition.

muckrakers (MUK-rayk-erz) A term used to describe writers and journalists who exposed the problems of America's industrial society.

National Consumers' League (NAH-shuh-nul kun-SOO-merz LEEG) An organization founded in 1899 to place limits on the amount of hours per week that women and children could work and to increase the minimum wage.

New Deal (NOO DEEL) The legislative program of President Franklin D. Roosevelt designed to promote economic recovery and social reform during the 1930s.

reformer (rih-FORM-er) A person who works for positive changes in politics, government, or society.

segregation (seh-gruh-GAY-shun) The act of keeping people of one race, sex, or social class apart from others.

slum (SLUM) A populated urban area marked by crowding, rundown housing, and poverty.

Standard Oil (STAN-derd OYL) A monopolistic oil company founded by John D. Rockefeller that controlled the production, refinement, and transport of oil in the United States during the early nineteenth century.

tenement (TEN-uh-ment) A building with many floors and with many families living on each level.

Web Sites

Due to the changing nature of Internet links, the Rosen Publishing Group, Inc., has developed an online list of Web sites related to the subject of this book. This site is updated regularly. Please use this link to access the list:

http://www.rosenlinks.com/pmnhnt/seho

Primary Source Image List

Page 5: This gelatin silver print was photographed by Lewis Wickes Hine in 1905. It is housed in the George Eastman Archive in Rochester, New York.

Page 6: The rear of a tenement apartment in Chicago can be seen in this nineteenth-century photograph. It is part of the Jane Addams Memorial Collection at the University of Illinois, Chicago.

Page 8: Jacob A. Riis captured this image of an illegal immigrants' lodging on Bayard Street in New York City in 1890. It is part of the permanent collection of the U.S. Library of Congress in Washington, D.C.

Page 10: An anonymous photographer recorded this lively scene on Hester Street in New York City in 1903. It is now part of the permanent collection of the U.S. National Archives.

Page 13: The photograph of Toynbee Hall was reprinted from *The Woman's Book, Vol. 2,* published by Charles Scribner and Sons, 1894. It is housed at Duke University in Durham, North Carolina.

Page 13 (inset): An anonymous photographer took this photograph of Samuel Augustus Barnett and Henrietta Barnett in 1910. It is now part of the Rischgitz Collection of Getty Images in New York.

Page 14: This lithograph of an American Red Cross public health nurse was created by Gordon Grant between 1914 and 1918 and is now part of the permanent collection of the U.S. Library of Congress, in Washington, D.C..

Page 15: An anonymous photographer took this image of one of Chicago's Hull House nurseries in the 1890s. It is housed at Swarthmore College in Swarthmore, Pennsylvania.

Page 17: This undated anonymous portrait of Jane Addams is part of the permanent collection of historical photographs at Swarthmore College in Swarthmore, Pennsylvania.

Page 19: The women in this photograph were studying at Wellesley Colege in 1886. It was taken from the Wellesley College Archives, Wellesley, Massachusetts.

Page 21: This pamphlet describing the duties and responsibilities of the Phillis Wheatley Home Association Board of Trustees is part of the collection of the Western Reserve Historical Society of Cleveland, Ohio.

Page 23: This anonymous 1909 photograph of a female public health nurse is part of the archives of the Visiting Nurse Service of New York.

Page 24: Eleanor Roosevelt is pictured in this anonymous photograph taken on December 1, 1932, in New York City.

Page 26: Lewis Wickes Hine took the photographs that make up this public service advertisement from the early 1900s. It is now housed at the U.S. Library of Congress in Washington, D.C.

Page 27: Women suffragists are seen in this anonymous photograph taken on February 9, 1913, that advertises a public talk about the suffrage movement at New York's Carnegie Hall.

Index

A
Abbott, Edith, 26
Abbott, Grace, 26
Addams, Jane, 14, 16, 22
African American settlement houses, 20
American Red Cross, 25
Andover House (South End House), 12–14

B
Barnett, Samuel A., 12
Breckinridge, Sophonisba, 26

C
Carnegie Steel, 4
child labor, 7, 11, 20, 24
Civil War, 4, 11
Coit, Stanton, 12
College Settlement, 12

D
disease, 6, 7, 14

G
Goodman, Benny, 16
Great Depression, 11

H
Hamilton, Alice, 26
Henry Street Settlement, 14, 22
Hopkins, Harry, 26
Hull, Charles, 16

H
Hull House, 14, 16, 20, 22, 26
Hunter, Jane, 20

I
Immigrants' Protective League, 26

J
jobs, 4, 7, 15

K
Kelley, Florence, 25

L
Lathrop, Julia, 2

N
National Consumers' League, 25
Negro Fellowship League, 20
Neighborhood Guild (University Settlement), 12
Nineteenth Amendment, 11

P
Perkins, Frances, 26
Phillis Wheatley Home, 20
Progressive Era/movement, 9, 11

R
reformers, 9, 11
Riis, Jacob A., 7
Roosevelt, Eleanor, 25, 26
Roosevelt, Franklin D., 11, 25, 26

S
settlement house residents, 17, 21, 23, 24–25, 26, 27
social work, 16, 26

About the Authors

Michael Friedman is the author of nearly sixty fiction and nonfiction books for children and adults. He received an undergraduate degree in communications from the Newhouse School at Syracuse University. This is Brett Friedman's first book.